FIRST TO THE TOP OF THE WORLD:

Admiral Peary at the North Pole

By Tom Lisker

Illustrated by Gloria Priam

cpi
contemporary perspectives, inc.

Library of Congress Number 78-14924

Art and Photo Credits
Cover illustration, Gloria Priam
Photos on pages 21, 41 and 44, UPI
Every effort has been made to trace the ownership of all
copyrighted material in this book and to obtain permission for
its use.

Library of Congress Cataloging in Publication Data

Lisker, Tom, 1928-
First to the top of the world: Admiral Peary at the North Pole

SUMMARY: A biography of the man whose dream of being
the first man to set foot on the North Pole became reality.
1. Peary, Robert Edwin, 1856-1920 — Juvenile literature. 2.
North Pole — Juvenile literature. 3. Explorers — United States
— Biography — Juvenile literature. [1. Peary, Robert Edwin,
1856-1920. 2. Explorers] I. Title.
G635.P4L5   919.8'040924 [B] [92]   78-14924
ISBN 0-89547-047-0

Manufactured in the United States of America
ISBN 0-89547-047-0

Contents

Chapter 1
THE RACE IS ON

On April 6, 1909 six cold and weary men planted an American flag in a block of ice. Four of them — Eskimos — cheered loudly. Their dogs barked, frightened by the sudden noise. Except for the freezing cold winds around them, there was not another sound.

Nowhere else, as far as the eye could see, was there anything but ice. Not a person, not an animal, not a building. Just a bare, frozen, silent world of ice.

Everyone in the group now looked from the flag to the two men — one black, the other white — who had just planted it in the ice. It had taken these two more than 23 years to reach this cold, bare land. They had suffered much. They had failed many times before, but now they had done the "impossible." They were the first to have made it all the way to the top of the world. They were the first to reach the North Pole.

5

The story of these men and their unbelievable-but-true adventure really began over 2,000 years ago. In those times, most thinking people in Europe no longer believed the earth was flat. But even if it were round, they thought if a ship sailed south from Europe it would get too close to the sun. The rocks in the sea would be red hot. The ocean water would be boiling. The crew would not be able to withstand the heat. So sailing too far south meant certain death. The ancient people called this the "burning zone." Today we call it the *Torrid Zone.*

People in ancient times also thought ships could not go too far north from Europe. If they did, the crew would freeze to death. They called the far north the "frozen zone." Today we call it the *Frigid Zone.*

For hundreds and hundreds of years the Europeans went on believing they had to stay in the middle — between the far north and the far south — to stay alive. Today we call this "middle" the *Temperate Zone.* But along came someone who was smart enough to change that kind of thinking.

Around 1430 Prince Henry of Portugal sent some ships along the west coast of Africa. They sailed farther and farther south into the Atlantic Ocean. And they were neither burned nor boiled alive. After the prince's ships found some beautiful islands, sailors dared to go even farther south — to the equator. Still,

Most people in Europe thought that parts of the ocean were boiling hot. ▶

no one saw the ocean boil. It was a little warmer than it was at home, that was all.

In the southern waters were lands where green things grew beautifully. People lived there quite happily. Now all over Europe ships were sailing in every direction to see what new lands they could find. Christopher Columbus was one of those explorers.

It was not until 400 years after Columbus that the North Pole was found. It was not that people weren't interested in finding it before then. Explorers had been searching after it for years, but it was not just the North Pole they were after. They wanted a faster way to sail from Europe over the top of the world to the Orient. There they would find the lands of spices and wealth. The Europeans had the right idea. The trip over the North Pole *is* the shortest and fastest way to the Orient. Today airplanes fly that way all the time. The early explorers had not yet found the way north by land or sea. But by 1906 some were getting closer to the North Pole. The race across the ice was on.

Chapter 2

TWO MEN AND ONE DREAM

No one ever worked harder to become famous than Robert E. Peary (pronounced Peery). He was born in Cresson, Pennsylvania, on May 6, 1856. Even as a child, he dreamed of making his name known around the world. He was fired with one burning hope — that someday he would be the first to do something big and important.

Peary was a fine student and a very strong young man. He loved nature and outdoor life. In Maine, where he grew up, he spent much of his time hunting and fishing and walking through the woods. Young Peary also had a great love of adventure. He often talked of someday standing alone in a place where no one had ever stood before. He said he wanted to see what no one had ever seen before.

Peary claimed he once had a dream that he would be the first man to set foot on the North Pole. He decided to make this dream his life goal, and he never gave up on that goal for 23 years. In that time he made eight

Robert Peary said he had a dream — he would be first to the North Pole.

different trips to the frozen north. He lost his toes because of the freezing cold. He broke his leg and came close to death several times. But always he went on trying to make his dream come true — to be the first to the pole. Peary came a little closer to the goal when he met Matthew Henson.

Matthew Henson was born in 1866. Although slavery had just ended, Matt's parents had never been slaves. Henson grew up in Washington, D.C., where he went to elementary school. But when he was 13 Henson was a cabin boy on a ship sailing to China.

Matthew Henson was a cabin boy sailing to China when he was 13.

By the time Henson returned home, sailing was in his blood. He became a sailor and soon came to know almost every large port in the world. He was smart and strong — a good seaman. More important, he was the kind of man you could trust with your life. No one would come to know this better than Robert Peary.

When he was 21 Henson began working with Peary. Peary was then a lieutenant in the United States Navy. Although Henson started as a messenger, it wasn't long before he became Peary's right-hand man.

Peary planned and raised money for the trips. But Henson did just about everything else. He hired the Eskimos, chose the dogs, and built the dog sleds (called sledges). He became as good as an Eskimo in hunting, building igloos, and living in the freezing cold of the far north.

The story of the first trip to the top of the world is the story of these two men — Robert E. Peary and Matthew Henson. Once these men met they formed a friendship that would hold them together for more than 20 years.

Robert Peary was a civil engineer. He then joined the United States Navy and became an officer. At that time the United States was planning a canal that would join the Atlantic and Pacific Oceans. Such a canal would shorten the time and distance for people like Henson who sailed from the east coast to the west

Peary cut through the thick jungle of Nicaragua.

coast of North America or on to the Orient. The canal might be built in one of two countries — Nicaragua or Panama. One of Peary's first jobs in the navy was to help plan the canal.

For three long, hard months, Peary lived and worked in the forests and swamps of Nicaragua. To get from place to place he had to cut through thick jungle.

Much of the time he walked through swamp waters up to his neck. His nights were spent in the fields with a few palm leaves to cover him as he slept.

All the time Peary worked in the jungle, he never stopped thinking about the other end of the world — the Arctic. As soon as he got back to Washington, D.C., he began reading everything he could find about the far north. He was hungry for stories about people who had already visited there. He wanted to know the problems they ran into — he would not make the same mistakes. Aside from his dream as a young man, there was no reason for Peary to try getting to the North Pole. He had no money or support. He had never set foot on the Arctic wastelands. Yet something inside him drove him there. Something that said, *be the first to do it!*

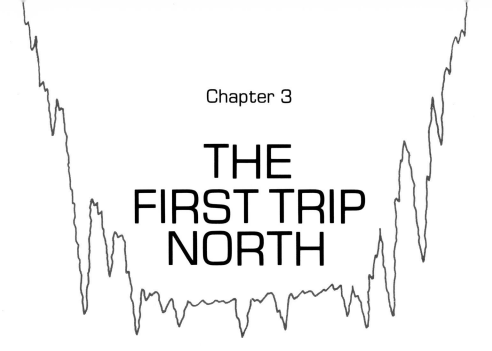

Chapter 3

THE FIRST TRIP NORTH

In 1886 Peary asked the navy for a six month leave. He also asked his mother for a loan of $500. He got both and he started at once for Greenland.

Peary was not trying to reach the North Pole. He was making this trip simply to learn as much as he could about the Arctic. He wanted to find answers that no one had at that time. Was Greenland a separate island or part of the land that went to the North Pole? Could he some day reach the North Pole by crossing Greenland? Since no one knew how to get to the North Pole, Peary would have to find the way himself. He would also test some of his ideas and equipment. What tools would he need when he made the *big* trip?

15

Peary planned a sled that curved up at its front. It was going to have to ride over snowdrifts. It had to be strong enough to carry a load of about 200 pounds. But it also had to be light enough for him to be able to pull it by himself.

Hard as it may be to believe, Robert Peary was going to make this first trip into Greenland alone. But at his jumping-off point — a place called Ritenbank — he met a young Dane named Christian Maigaard. Maigaard became so excited about Peary's plans to cross the lands of ice that he decided to join him.

Peary and Maigaard found the frozen north filled with all the dangers they had heard about and more. The two faced terrible blizzards. The snowfalls were so thick that there were times when they could not see in any direction. Bitter cold winds blew across the endless sea of ice.

Among the worst dangers were the crevasses — great, deep cracks in the polar ice. Some were narrow enough to jump across. But others were as wide as 50 feet. To add to the danger these wide cracks were often hidden by snow.

Peary and Maigaard would have to move clear around the deep crevasses, adding many more miles to their travels. Or they would move slowly over bridges of snow that crossed the crevasses. One at a time they would crawl across, praying these snow bridges would hold the weight of their sledges.

Most of the time Peary and Maigaard were tied together by a rope as they moved around. It was one way to keep each man from losing the other in the heavy, blinding snow. But there came a moment when the rope was used to save Maigaard's life.

They were circling a large, deep crevass one day. Maigaard suddenly lost his footing. He found one leg hanging in a deep crack in the ice that had been hidden by snow. When Peary felt a sudden pull on his rope he knew Maigaard was in trouble. Peary grabbed a chunk of ice jutting up from the snow. He hung on with all his might, hoping the ice would not break away in his hand.

Meanwhile, Maigaard had no idea how deep the crack was. He only knew the rope that tied him to Peary was keeping him from falling any further into the crack. But would the rope hold? Could Peary, somewhere out there in the snow, keep holding him up? Slowly Maigaard pulled on the rope trying to move up out of the crevass. He inched his way through the snow, feeling for any rough edge of ice he could pull on.

Maigaard's gloved hand felt something hard under the snow. It was a small bump of ice. He pulled at it. It held. Now, with all his might and with the help of Peary's rope, he pulled himself up and away from the crevass. Peary's rope and cool head had kept Maigaard from a long fall and certain death.

Greenland was like no place Peary could have imagined. In his notes he called it "an Arctic Sahara." And in a way it *was* like a desert. There were no animals. There were no plants. There was no rock or soil anywhere to be seen. Only the snow on the frozen plain, the cold blue sky, and the cold white sun.

When Peary and Maigaard had gone about 100 miles from where they started, they had just enough food left for six more days. It was time to turn around and head for home. The two would soon say goodbye to each other, but they were happy men. They had done what they had set out to do. They had gone farther across Greenland than anyone before them.

◄ With Peary's help Maigaard slowly climbed from the crevass.

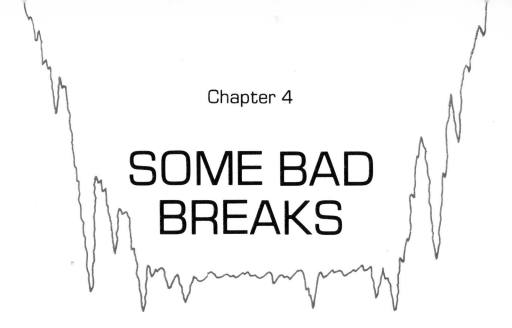

Chapter 4

SOME BAD BREAKS

The following year, Peary returned to Nicaragua. He worked hard and took little rest. But, oddly enough, he was *happy*. He was doing his job in a part of the world very few had ever seen before. For now, that would be his only joy. The canal, of course, was never built through Nicaragua. It went through Panama, and Peary's ideas and plans were never used. It was later found out that his plan would have saved the United States 16 miles of canal building and $17 million.

But Peary would always remember the trip with a smile. It was on this trip that Peary got to know Matthew Henson. They worked together, they planned together, and they talked for hours at a time. The dream of being first to the North Pole was now shared by two men — Robert Peary and Matthew Henson.

Upon his return home, Peary was married. Although he seemed to settle down for awhile, his thoughts were never very far from the Arctic. He was paid to give talks about his trip to Greenland. With this money and the money given by others who believed in him, Peary was ready for another trip north.

This time he planned to sail as far north as he could, set up a base camp, and spend the winter in Greenland. Then he would continue across the ice to the northeast the following spring and summer.

In June, 1891, Peary sailed from New York on a ship named the *Kite*. There were six others with him — Matthew Henson, Eivind Astrup, Dr. Frederick Cook, Langdon Gibson, John Verhoeff, and one more, Peary's wife, Jo. Many Americans were surprised to find that Mrs. Peary would make such a trip. And many were upset that she should do such a thing while she was pregnant.

As the little *Kite* sailed north through icy waters, Jo and Robert Peary often stood on deck. They liked watching the ship as it worked its way around the larger icebergs or cut right through the thinner ice. It was all very thrilling and, by now, Jo Peary was fired with the same dream her husband had.

One day, while standing on deck, Peary was badly hurt. The ship suddenly hit a large piece of ice and for a moment was thrown from side to side. An iron bar smashed against the wheelhouse where Peary stood. He was hit hard and broke his leg just above the ankle. The break was bad and Peary was in a lot of pain.

For a while Peary's friends wanted to turn back. "I won't let you do that," cried Peary. "We must go ahead!" Afraid they might turn back anyway, he slept with a compass next to his bed. That way he could always be sure of the direction in which the ship was sailing. Nothing would stop Peary — not a broken leg or some well-meaning friends.

22   Peary fell to the deck of the wheelhouse, his leg broken. ▶

Peary couldn't move from his bed, but his wife helped him to see what was happening on deck. She opened a space in the wall above his bed and hung a mirror there. She tilted the mirror so that he could see the deck. It worked something like a periscope. It probably didn't work very well, but it gave Peary some idea of what was going on.

By the end of July, the *Kite* made it to Whale Sound. There Peary was strapped to a board and lowered into a small boat. He was rowed to shore and carried to his tent. From his bed he watched the building of Red Cliff, their snug base camp house. Meanwhile the *Kite* sailed for home.

Everything Peary had read — all that he had learned from his earlier trip to the Arctic — told him that he had to live as the Eskimos did. He wore Eskimo clothes and ate Eskimo foods. He copied their way of life — even living in the igloos, or snow houses, that the Eskimos built. Peary figured that the Eskimos were the best teachers he could find on how to live in the Arctic.

That first long Arctic winter was as important to Matt Henson as it was to Robert Peary. Henson would learn as much as he could about Eskimo life. He learned the language and made many Eskimo friends. He even adopted a young Eskimo boy whose mother

Henson learned to travel and live as an Eskimo. ▶

had died just before the group had landed. Henson also learned how to drive a team of dogs, build an igloo, and repair the sledges.

As Peary's leg got better he tested it on a few short trips north. Even with two good legs it wasn't a good idea to go any great distance during the Arctic winter. The sun doesn't come out much during the winter months. When you are that far north from the Equator the winter days are very short. In the Arctic winter there are some days when the sun never shines at all. In the North Pole winter there is no sun for six months. But in the summer the sun shines day and night. The Peary group would have to sit out the Arctic winter and its darkness.

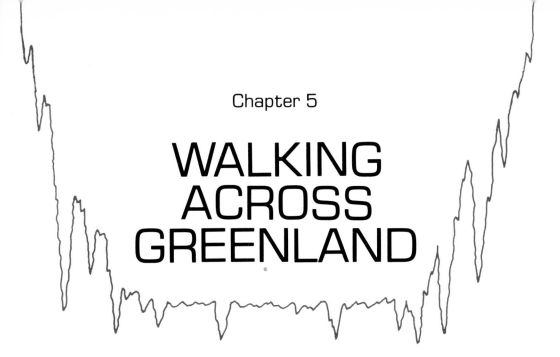

Chapter 5

WALKING ACROSS GREENLAND

By May there was enough sunlight and Peary got his group on the move. They tried not to carry too much with them. They carried no tents — only what they needed in the way of food, supplies, and equipment. They took only one rifle and one box of cartridges. They would sleep in snow houses that they would build when needed. Jo stayed back at Red Cliff.

Only four men went north. Peary did not want too many men to go. More men would mean more food and more supplies. Two men would turn back after the first couple of weeks. That would leave only two to move on to the Greenland coast. *If there was such a coast.* Peary thought that Greenland must be an island, but he could not be sure. Many others thought Greenland stretched all the way to the North Pole. Since nobody had ever been there, no one really knew.

Toward the end of May, the first two men were sent back. That left Peary and Eivind Astrup to walk on into the unknown. With their dog teams they moved slowly northward — through storms, deep snows, and over slippery ice. Often the men actually climbed into the straps that held the dogs. Straining with all their might, they helped the dogs pull the sledges through the snow.

On July 4th, with food running low, Peary and Astrup reached what looked to them like the end of Greenland. Far below them they saw a body of water. It led northwest to the Arctic Ocean. Because of the day on which they discovered it, Peary named the bay Independence Bay. That is one of the great joys of being an explorer—when you are the first person to get someplace, you can name it whatever you want. Over the years Peary named many places he was the first to see. Often he named them for the people who gave him the most money for his trips. They liked this very much and could be counted on for help with Peary's next trips.

Worn out, cold, and hungry, Peary and Astrup started back for Red Cliff — more than 500 miles away. It would be a hard trip, and not only because of the ice and blizzards. They would have to be very careful about moving in the right direction. They were so close to the North Pole that their compass would not work well. They would need to keep checking or

◀ The men had to help the dogs pull the sledges over ice.   29

"reading" the sun's position to be sure of the way back. But the weather was so stormy that Peary could take only three readings of the sun in the whole month they traveled. He had to follow his hunches about where north and south were — what they call "dead reckoning." Even with all these problems the two men returned to a spot within five miles of their base camp.

Peary had some very bad news waiting for him at Red Cliff. One of the two men he sent back at the end of May was missing. John Verhoeff had become lost in a blinding snowstorm. It was believed he fell to his death in a crevass. No sign of him was ever found.

By the time the *Kite* had picked up Peary's group and was sailing home, Robert Peary was planning his next trip north. He was now certain he could reach the North Pole by way of Greenland. It would be easier this time because he had already crossed Greenland. And he had Matt Henson. Henson had learned the Eskimo ways so well that he could live like one easily. And he was teaching Peary how to stay alive on the northern ice.

Raising money for the new trip would be easier, too. Peary was well known. People wanted to meet him and hear what he had to say. He would show people the things that he used for cooking, living, and traveling in the north. Poor Matt Henson would perspire in his Arctic furs as he stood in front of the crowd to show them what they wore. Once in a while

Peary and Henson raised money by telling people of their
adventures in the Arctic.

Peary would speak too long. Then the dogs would howl
and that would end the talk.

Peary also came up with a new way to make more
money. He decided to sail in a larger ship — the
Falcon. To raise money, he let people all along the
East Coast come on board for twenty-five cents a person.
The money poured in. And the *Falcon* headed north.

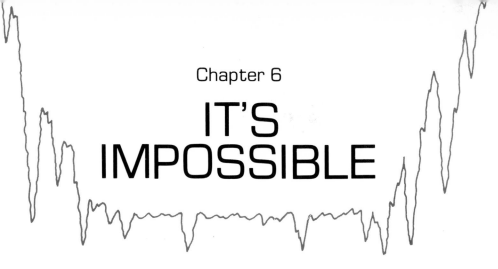

Chapter 6

IT'S IMPOSSIBLE

Problems began to pile up for Peary and Henson right from the start. Sickness, bad weather, and accidents came one after another on this trip to Greenland. The weather was so bad Peary wanted everyone to go home. He would stay in Greenland for another year. But Matt Henson and Hugh Lee refused to leave. The three made the trip to Independence Bay, but it was as far as they could go. They did not have enough food and almost starved to death. Finally, they were forced to turn back.

There were many trips to the north before Peary's and Henson's. All had ended very unhappily. The Franklin group left from England on two ships in 1845. Every man was lost. The De Long group sailed to the Arctic in 1879 on the ship *Jeanette*. They were trapped between ice packs for two years. In time more ice formed around the ship crushing it and killing all but a few of the men aboard. In 1881 the Greely expedition of 33 men returned home with only 6 men still alive. It was even said that some of the men may have eaten the bodies of their shipmates to stay alive.

Peary knew how many others had tried to reach the pole and failed. It told him how lucky he was to even be alive. Still, Peary was disappointed. "Yes, I am happy to still be alive," he told Jo, "but I still haven't made it to the pole!" Yet Peary and Henson knew they had learned something on this trip that would make the next one easier. *The way to the pole was not across the Greenland ice cap.*

There were other reasons for Peary to be happy. On his return, the American Geographic Society and the Royal Geographic Society of London gave him medals. Peary was becoming known all over the country, with all the news stories about the trip. A group had been formed that later became the Peary Arctic Club. Its members gave Peary a ship and the money for his next trip to the pole.

Within a few years Peary, Henson, and Dr. T.S. Dedrick, Jr. were again headed north to the land of snow, ice, Eskimos, and the big goal — the North Pole. On this trip, their ship would try to push its way through the icy channel between Greenland and Ellesmere Island. That way he could save several hundred miles of sledging overland.

Peary's new ship, the *Windward*, never got as far north as they had hoped. It became locked in ice far to the south of where they had planned to go. The only hope left was to unload the ship and head north by sledge. "Let's see if we can reach Fort Conger," said Peary. "That should be about 250 miles from here."

The three men headed for Fort Conger in 50 degrees-below-zero weather. Four Eskimos joined them. It was the Arctic winter — the most dangerous time for travel. They had only the moon for light. And in two weeks the moonlight would be gone.

The men felt their way through the darkness of the Arctic night.

The ice grew worse as they made their way along the shore of Ellesmere Island. There were freezing winds and heavy snows. As the days of moonlight ran out they covered less and less ground. The weak light of the moon finally gave way to no light at all. But there was nothing they could do but keep going on.

The men and the dogs slowly felt their way in the darkness through the sea of ice. After several days they came upon a low, snow-covered building. They pushed their way inside. It was Fort Conger. It was *safety*.

No one had been in the building in 15 years. Once inside, the Peary group found some coffee in an open can. They found that by using a lot of it, it didn't taste too bad. Now, with a fire going and without freezing winds biting at them, the three men sat quietly. They thought about the 27 other men who had never returned from Fort Conger.

Later, as they talked, Peary had a strange feeling in his feet. He took off his boots. His toes had been very badly frozen. After a few hours of pain, he found his toes had an odd color. He asked Dr. Dedrick to look at them. One look at the doctor's eyes told Peary the story. Dr. Dedrick had to cut off seven of Peary's toes, then and there. It was the worst time of Peary's life. He was 200 miles from the *Windward*. He and his two friends were closed in by snow, storm, and night. He

wondered whether he would ever be able to walk again. But that night he wrote on the wall beside his bed: *"I shall find a way or make one."*

For six weeks Peary could not stand without help. He was taken back to the *Windward*, tied to a sledge. When he got there Dr. Dedrick had to cut off another of Peary's toes. Only the little toe on each foot was left. Yet little more than one month later Peary and Henson were back at Fort Conger. They were going to move farther north, or die trying.

Peary and Henson, now by themselves, traveled 400 miles along the North Greenland coast. They reached places that no one had ever seen. They never got anywhere near the North Pole but they did learn what it was like to cross the ice of the Arctic Ocean. Finally, more than two years after they had left the *Windward*, they once again sailed home.

Now Peary's hopes were crumbling. Another trip north, another failure! Sad and suddenly feeling very old, Peary wrote: *"My dream of 16 years is ended. I have made a good fight, but I cannot accomplish the impossible."*

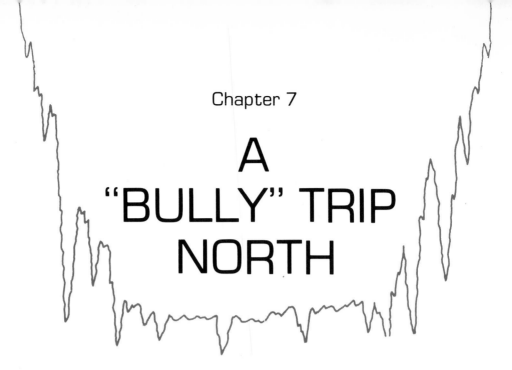

Chapter 7

A "BULLY" TRIP NORTH

Impossible or not, three years later Peary and Henson went north again. This time it was with the help of many more people. One person who helped was the president of the United States, Theodore Roosevelt. Peary planned to build a new ship that would push its way through the ice to the Arctic Ocean. He named her the *Roosevelt*.

In 1905 the *Roosevelt* sailed farther north than any other ship had ever gone. They got up as far as Cape Sheridan. From there the explorers headed north across the Arctic Ocean. All aboard were sure this was it — the last leg to the North Pole.

Peary once again set out for the North Pole.

But once again they had to turn back before they reached their goal. This time they were stopped by another great danger — the Arctic *leads*. These are great openings of sea water in the ice that sometimes stretch for miles. They make travel by foot or sled impossible. They could not wait for the leads to freeze over because food and time would have run out. So, disappointed for the seventh time, Robert E. Peary, Matt Henson, and their crew sadly headed for home.

The two explorers had come too close this time to give up now. Two years later the *Roosevelt* was once again ready to sail. President Teddy Roosevelt came aboard the ship to wish them all good luck. "Bully!" he cried, as he patted Peary on the back. Then he shook hands with each of the men who would sail with Peary — Henson, Ross, Marvin, George Borup, Donald MacMillan, Dr. J.W. Goodsell, and "Captain Bob" Bartlett.

The *Roosevelt* pushed her way back to Cape Sheridan. The explorers made the 93-mile sail to Cape Columbia in four days. There they set up camp. They were now just 413 miles from the North Pole.

This trip north was the best planned of all. "Forward march!" The order from Peary started the forward party moving farther northward. Captain Bartlett led the way with his crew and sledge. George Borup was the scout. Three days later all the others started north with Henson in the lead. They were following the trail Bartlett had made.

Twenty-four men, 19 sledges, and 123 dogs marched along an icy trail that could become snow covered at any time. It was so cold that the brandy Peary carried under his coat froze solid.

They camped in the igloos Bartlett and Borup had made. Early in the morning they would break camp. Henson's team would follow Bartlett's trail. The rest would follow Henson. Peary brought up the rear. He was saving his energy for the final dash.

President Teddy Roosevelt came aboard the ship to wish them good luck.

After just two days, a dark cloud appeared. It was
the kind that floats over open water on the Arctic
Ocean. Sure enough, Henson came to a lead about a
quarter of a mile wide. But it was not going to stop
them this time. They would get across this lead on
floating ice. They could easily have lost their lives in
the freezing waters, but they made it.

Another two days found them again halted — this
time by the Big Lead. It stretched for miles. For one
week, Henson and Peary waited unhappily while the
food supplies ran out. MacMillan thought up games
to keep the men busy. Then, as the lead froze over,
they crossed it. And they crossed seven others on
their march north.

Food was running out. Peary started sending small
groups back to base camp. The first to go was Dr.

Goodsell. Then MacMillan. After five more days, Borup was sent back and then Ross Marvin. No one knew when or how it happened, but Professor Marvin lost his life at the Big Lead on his return trip.

Peary and Henson went on, following the trail made by Bartlett. They had been on the ocean for almost a month. *Now they were only 180 miles from the pole.*

Once again they came to a lead. And once again they had to wait. Bartlett awoke one morning to find his group drifting away from Peary and Henson and into a big lead. Luckily they were able to jump to safety as the ice drifted back close to where the others were.

A few days later Bartlett was sent back, but by then he had gone farther north than any other person in history. Now only Robert Peary, Matthew Henson, and the four Eskimos were left. For five more days they pressed their way forward. Once Henson fell into the freezing waters of a lead. Ootah, one of the Eskimos, leaped into the water and saved him. Moments later they were marching forward — moving, moving all the time.

On April 6, 1909 the six men stopped and made camp. Peary took readings from the sun while Henson and the Eskimos built the igloos. The land of ice was still — so quiet that it would have been hard to tell that Robert E. Peary and Matthew Henson had just done the impossible. They had reached their dream. They were standing at the North Pole!

Henson stepped forward with a big smile on his face. Feeling the time had come, he took off his glove meaning to shake Peary's hand. But Peary's eyes must have been burning from lack of sleep. He pressed his hands over his eyes and never even saw Henson's hand. He simply turned and headed toward his igloo to get some sleep. Later on, Peary said that he was too tired at the time to even know that his life's dream had come true.

After a short rest Peary took several more readings from the sun. He wanted to make very, very sure that they were really at the top of the world. He took two Eskimos — Egingwah and Seegloo — ten miles farther for more readings. At last he was satisfied. They had indeed reached the North Pole.

Peary took a picture of his men, a picture that was to become famous. He took one long look at the flag he had planted in the ice. It was waving in the breeze. Then with the others he headed back to the *Roosevelt* and the long but happy trip home. *He had been the first. He had seen what no one had ever seen before.*

A FINAL WORD

Before closing the pages on Robert Peary's "first," something else must be said. Peary, who had been disappointed many times, had one more sad moment when he came home from the pole.

A New York doctor, Frederick A. Cook, claimed that he, not Peary, had been first to the North Pole. The doctor said he had been there one year before Peary and had only just returned. For the rest of his life, Cook stuck to his story. There are many who still believe that story.

Peary was never angrier than he was with Cook. He called Dr. Cook a liar and would not share the honor with him when Cook offered to do so. Most scientists have since decided that Peary's photographs and scientific reports of the North Pole prove he was first. But for many years Peary was a broken man. He felt cheated of what he wanted most. Not money, but glory — the glory of being *first*.